101 STORY STARTERS for Teens

by

Maisy Day

BATCH OF BOOKS

batchofbooks.com

ISBN: 9798646440885
Text copyright © 2020 Dena McMurdie. All rights reserved.

Published by Batch of Books.

Interior design and cover design by Dena McMurdie.

Cover art by ikopylove, Softulka, and MisterElements.

First printing, May 2020.

Table of Contents

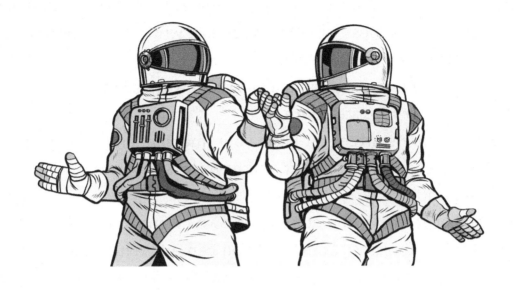

How to Use This Book........................... 4

Science Fiction 5

Fantasy.......................................19

Mystery and Thrillers.........................33

Humor.......................................47

Historical Fiction.............................61

Realistic Fiction..............................75

Horror.......................................89

Romance....................................101

How to Use This Book:

Whether you've got a creative writing assignment for school, want a warm-up exercise, or are looking for short story inspiration, you're in the right place. This book contains over one hundred first lines for stories in eight different genres. So it doesn't matter if you like writing science fiction, humor, or romance, we've got you covered.

Using this book is super simple. Just follow these steps:

1. Locate your favorite genre.
2. Find a story starter that kicks your imagination into high gear.
3. Decide what happens next and how the story ends.
4. Start writing!

Remember to make the story your own. Want to change a character's name, gender, or ethnicity? Go ahead! You can add extra characters, change the setting, and switch up the point-of-view. You can alter anything about it that you want. How you write your stories is 100% up to you. So use your imagination and make the story as unique as you are.

Some Writing Tips:

- Give your character a backstory. Every good character needs a past and it's up to you to make one up for your story. This will help your character feel like a real person.
- Your character needs a problem to solve. This book will help you start your story, but you'll need to figure out what your character is working toward and what obstacles they have to face along the way.
- Give your story a beginning, a middle, and an end. You need all three for your story to work.
- Practice makes perfect. The more stories you write, the better you will get at it. Don't worry if your first story isn't a masterpiece. Keep writing and you'll keep improving.

What are you waiting for? Turn the page and get writing!

SCIENCE

FICTION

The room was filled with identical humans standing at attention in perfect rows. Their eyes stared blankly ahead as they waited for orders.

The virtual reality game promised to be the experience of a lifetime.

Three agents in hazmat suits pinned me down while a fourth injected a serum into my neck.

I had always dreamed of exploring the galaxy and I wasn't about to miss my chance.

The room shifted into focus as I blinked away the years of cryo-sleep. A woman stood over me with a tablet, taking notes.

"What year is it?" I asked.

The robot was so lifelike, I didn't immediately realize it wasn't human.

When the government asked for volunteers to settle a newly terraformed planet, I didn't hesitate to sign up.

The first time I saw a genetically modified human, I couldn't take my eyes off of her.

I'd never been to Earth before. I tried to imagine what it would feel like when I set my feet on solid ground for the first time.

I could see the planet in the distance, dream-like as it hung among the stars. Nothing could have prepared me for what happened next.

_____

_____

_____

_____

_____

_____

_____

_____

_____

_____

_____

_____

_____

_____

_____

_____

_____

_____

The Z Games Championship was the biggest gaming competition in the world. It attracted the best players from across the globe. This year, I was going to win.

I created the app for a school assignment. I never expected it to change the world.

"Hold on!" The pilot's panicked voice was a stark contrast against the calm of the stars. "This could get rough."

I had spent a decade in hiding, surviving on the charity of others. But I was finished with the pity I saw in people's eyes. Finished with begging for every scrap of bread. It was time to become the queen my people needed.

The magic built in my veins until it hurt. I fought for control, but I knew it was a losing battle. It was only a matter of time before I couldn't contain it.

I focused on my reflection, making sure I got all the details right. The mole on the left cheek, the warm brown of the eyes. When I finished my transformation, my sister's face stared back at me.

Nobody expected the spell to work. After all, I was only a servant with almost no magical abilities.

"Welcome to the Academy of Magic." The man took my suitcase, folded it like a paper airplane, and tossed it into the air. It sailed around one of the dormitory towers before disappearing into a window. Smiling at my stunned expression, he ushered me through the massive double doors.

The forest loomed dark and foreboding in front of me. Legends of dark magic and curious creatures lurked in my mind, but turning back was not an option. I adjusted the strap of my pack and stepped into the trees.

If I had known how the book would change my life, I never would have picked it up.

_____

_____

_____

_____

_____

_____

_____

_____

_____

_____

_____

_____

_____

_____

_____

_____

Blue flames sparked in the boy's hands and danced across his fingers. He grinned when I took a step backward.

"What are you?" I demanded.

_____

_____

_____

_____

_____

_____

_____

_____

_____

_____

_____

_____

_____

_____

_____

_____

_____

_____

The old woman pressed the vibrant green stone into my palm. "This is yours now," she rasped. "Don't let me down."

_____

_____

_____

_____

_____

_____

_____

_____

_____

_____

_____

_____

_____

_____

_____

_____

This shouldn't be happening. Magic disappeared from the kingdom hundreds of years ago, but there was no other explanation for the strange events of the last few days.

The prophecy was as bizarre and cryptic as you'd expect from a century-old oracle.

_____

_____

_____

_____

_____

_____

_____

_____

_____

_____

_____

_____

_____

_____

_____

_____

_____

_____

The dragon turned its fiery gaze on me, paralyzing me with fear. I needed to find a way out of this situation—fast.

In the legend, the moonstone could heal any wound of the body, heart, or mind. Finding it was my final hope.

The detective leaned in close. "Just tell me the truth," she said.

But the truth was complicated. Too complicated. The truth wasn't what she wanted to hear. So I told her the only thing I could.

He warned me this day would come. I should have listened, but now it was too late for regrets.

_____

_____

_____

_____

_____

_____

_____

_____

_____

_____

_____

_____

_____

_____

_____

_____

_____

_____

_____

The day that the girl went missing was the worst day of my life.

Everyone says it was a terrible accident, but I know the truth.

_____

_____

_____

_____

_____

_____

_____

_____

_____

_____

_____

_____

_____

_____

_____

_____

_____

_____

_____

My brother disappeared the same day Alec showed up at school.

I picked up the note and opened it.

I know what you did.
I'm coming for you.
−X

I had no memories of that night, but everyone was acting differently toward me. I needed to find out what happened.

Nobody thought he was capable of doing such a terrible thing, but they didn't know him the way I did.

_____

_____

_____

_____

_____

_____

_____

_____

_____

_____

_____

_____

_____

_____

_____

_____

_____

_____

When I got to my bedroom, a thick cream envelope sat on my pillow. My name was scrawled across the front in old-fashioned calligraphy.

_____

_____

_____

_____

_____

_____

_____

_____

_____

_____

_____

_____

_____

_____

_____

_____

_____

_____

_____

I stumbled over something in the dark. I flipped on my phone's flashlight to see what it was.

Something was lying in the middle of the dark street. Through the rain, it almost looked human. Beside me, Ellie gasped.

_____

_____

_____

_____

_____

_____

_____

_____

_____

_____

_____

_____

_____

_____

_____

_____

_____

_____

Meet me behind the arcade @ 6

I was apprehensive about meeting Tate alone, but she was the only person willing to talk to me about the murders.

HUMOR

After the incident last week, I'd be happy if I never saw a goat again for the rest of my life.

BFFs are *supposed* to tell each other everything. They're *supposed* to have your back. Especially when you have a pair of underwear sticking out of the bottom of your pants.

_____

_____

_____

_____

_____

_____

_____

_____

_____

_____

_____

_____

_____

_____

_____

_____

_____

_____

_____

_____

_____

It didn't take long for people to notice me. Before I could mutter "It's not what it looks like," I had dozens of phones pointed in my direction.

It was the absolute worst time for my allergies to kick in. I stifled a groan and prayed that no one would notice. I wasn't that lucky.

You never know when a clown wig will come in handy. As it turns out, today was the perfect day to have a bundle of fake, rainbow-colored hair stashed in my locker.

Ms. Walker strutted into class wearing the craziest outfit I'd ever seen.

_____

_____

_____

_____

_____

_____

_____

_____

_____

_____

_____

_____

_____

_____

_____

_____

_____

_____

It was going to be the best senior prank ever. Everything went according to plan until Jeremiah let the pigeon loose.

I'm beginning to think that bird poop is a good look for me.

_____

_____

_____

_____

_____

_____

_____

_____

_____

_____

_____

_____

_____

_____

_____

_____

_____

_____

_____

I should have known better than to trust my dad's advice. He thinks sweatpants are the height of fashion and anchovies are "the bomb". Why did I think he could help me with something this important?

_____

_____

_____

_____

_____

_____

_____

_____

_____

_____

_____

_____

_____

_____

_____

_____

I stepped off the bus, feeling like a million bucks in my brand new kicks. Unfortunately, that feeling didn't last long. My sneaker caught on the curb and sent me flailing face-first into the pavement.

The birthday cake was the most terrifying thing I'd ever seen in my life.

_____

_____

_____

_____

_____

_____

_____

_____

_____

_____

_____

_____

_____

_____

_____

_____

_____

I was excited about the prospect of earning some extra cash. Then I saw the banana costume.

HISTORICAL FICTION

UNDERWOOD

I'll never forget the day I received my conscription letter. Even though I had anticipated it, nothing could have prepared me to see the words ORDER TO REPORT FOR INDUCTION written across the top of the page in bold type.

I arrived in California with weary legs and a heart full of hope. It would be hard work, but the promise of gold was too great to resist.

_____

_____

_____

_____

_____

_____

_____

_____

_____

_____

_____

_____

_____

_____

_____

_____

_____

_____

The stack of my grandmother's letters sat on my nightstand. I didn't know what they contained, but it was time to find out. I picked up the first one and started to read.

I'd never been to a speakeasy before. My parents staunchly supported the law of prohibition and would be furious to learn I had visited such a place.

My parents lost everything in the stock market crash. Everything, including our home and my inheritance, was gone. All we had left was our pride.

The mare was the most beautiful horse I had ever laid eyes on. I knew in an instant that she and I were meant for each other.

_____

_____

_____

_____

_____

_____

_____

_____

_____

_____

_____

_____

_____

_____

_____

_____

_____

_____

I took a deep breath and pulled open the door to the recruiting office. If I was lucky, the army wouldn't question my age.

_____

_____

_____

_____

_____

_____

_____

_____

_____

_____

_____

_____

_____

_____

_____

_____

_____

_____

My father was determined to be rid of me. He planned to marry me off to the next gentleman who came along, whether we were a suitable match or not.

I picked up the bag holding my meager possessions and boarded the train.

The new world was the most beautiful and terrifying thing I'd ever seen. It was a wild, untamed land that promised riches and danger in equal measure.

_____

_____

_____

_____

_____

_____

_____

_____

_____

_____

_____

_____

_____

_____

_____

_____

_____

_____

_____

_____

One day, I vowed, *I will be free—owned by no one.*

The wagon train had already left. We would have to move quickly if we wanted to catch up with them.

_____

_____

_____

_____

_____

_____

_____

_____

_____

_____

_____

_____

_____

_____

_____

_____

_____

_____

_____

_____

realistic fiction

It was going to be the best party of my senior year. I wasn't going to let anything, not even myself, ruin it.

When you're dying, every breath becomes a miracle.

I never expected to meet my best friend in the hospital.

Everyone else was excited to graduate and move away, but I couldn't imagine leaving. This town was my home.

_____

_____

_____

_____

_____

_____

_____

_____

_____

_____

_____

_____

_____

_____

_____

_____

_____

_____

They didn't bother us, and we didn't bother them.

That was the unspoken rule in our city. It wasn't official, but it kept the peace—until the night that everything changed.

"Want to skip class today?" Tabitha's grin was infectious. I wouldn't have been able to say no if I'd tried.

I thought it was going to be just another boring shift at the Pizza Palace. I was wrong.

I flipped through the pages, speechless. The notebook was filled with embarrassing and awful secrets about almost everyone at school.

This was it—the last game of my high school career. I stood next to my teammates, soaking in the roar of the crowd as the band started to play the national anthem.

_____

_____

_____

_____

_____

_____

_____

_____

_____

_____

_____

_____

_____

_____

_____

_____

_____

_____

The new kid looked like he'd rather be anywhere but here.

At my age, nobody expects to be adopted. The most I hoped for was to get through the rest of my time in foster care unscathed.

I picked up the large white envelope but didn't open it yet. Its contents could change my life forever.

I thought nobody could understand what it was like to be me. But that changed the day I met Daisy.

_____

_____

_____

_____

_____

_____

_____

_____

_____

_____

_____

_____

_____

_____

_____

_____

_____

_____

_____

HORROR

The zombie lurched toward me. I scrambled out of the way and grabbed the first thing that could be used as a weapon.

_____

_____

_____

_____

_____

_____

_____

_____

_____

_____

_____

_____

_____

_____

_____

_____

_____

_____

_____

_____

_____

"Derek?" I gasped. "I thought you were dead."

Derek took a step toward me. "I am."

Katie burst through the door, covered in blood and breathing hard. I dropped the flashlight and hurried over to her. Her hands were shaking.

"What happened?" I asked.

_____

_____

_____

_____

_____

_____

_____

_____

_____

_____

_____

_____

_____

_____

_____

_____

_____

_____

_____

As soon as I entered the room, I knew something was wrong. I turned around just in time to see the door slam behind me and hear a lock click into place.

_____

_____

_____

_____

_____

_____

_____

_____

_____

_____

_____

_____

_____

_____

_____

_____

_____

_____

_____

_____

_____

All of my siblings disappeared without a trace the day after they turned eighteen. When my two older brothers vanished, I thought they simply cut ties with the town and our family. But after my sister disappeared, I realized something sinister was going on.

My birthday was in two weeks and I needed to figure out what happened to my siblings before I shared their fate.

A pair of yellow eyes glowed in the dark. A low growl echoed through the damp room. I fumbled for my flashlight and switched it on.

_____

_____

_____

_____

_____

_____

_____

_____

_____

_____

_____

_____

_____

_____

_____

_____

_____

_____

_____

My mother taught me the fine art of necromancy.

"Don't dismiss the dead," she warned me. "They have more power than people think."

_____

_____

_____

_____

_____

_____

_____

_____

_____

_____

_____

_____

_____

_____

_____

_____

_____

_____

_____

The creature turned toward me, moonlight falling across its features. I choked back a scream and fumbled for my flashlight.

_____

_____

_____

_____

_____

_____

_____

_____

_____

_____

_____

_____

_____

_____

_____

_____

_____

_____

_____

My father had forbidden me from ever opening the door at the back of the cellar. Until today, I'd never had a reason to disobey his orders.

_____

_____

_____

_____

_____

_____

_____

_____

_____

_____

_____

_____

_____

_____

_____

_____

_____

_____

_____

_____

The abandoned house was cold and creaky, but we had nowhere else to go.

_____

_____

_____

_____

_____

_____

_____

_____

_____

_____

_____

_____

_____

_____

_____

_____

_____

_____

_____

The only sound was the footfall of heavy boots and the scrape of an ax across the floor.

"Come out, come out, wherever you are." The man's raspy voice sent chills down my spine. I held my breath and prayed he wouldn't look under the bed.

_____

_____

_____

_____

_____

_____

_____

_____

_____

_____

_____

_____

_____

_____

_____

_____

_____

_____

_____

_____

Our eyes met across the crowded cafeteria. When he smiled at me, everything else faded away.

The first time I saw her was in Chemistry class.

_____

_____

_____

_____

_____

_____

_____

_____

_____

_____

_____

_____

_____

_____

_____

_____

_____

_____

_____

He was the type of boy that made girls go weak in the knees. I knew I didn't have a chance with him, but that didn't stop me.

He flashed a perfect smile and my heart sped up. When he laced our fingers together, all coherent thoughts fled my mind.

My phone pinged with a new notification. I smiled when I saw who it was from.

Prom was coming up fast and I still didn't have a date. I was getting desperate, which meant I was also getting reckless.

I didn't want to graduate high school without experiencing my first kiss. It was time to initiate Operation Pucker-Up.

My stomach did a flop when I saw him walking toward me. I didn't wait to find out if he'd seen my embarrassing note before I ducked into the girl's restroom to hide.

_____

_____

_____

_____

_____

_____

_____

_____

_____

_____

_____

_____

_____

_____

_____

_____

_____

_____

_____

_____

I knew he wasn't good for me, but that's what made him so irresistible.

Everyone knew that the girl on the motorbike was trouble. The problem was that no matter how hard I tried, I couldn't resist the promise of mischief. I took a deep breath and headed toward her.

The only open seat was next to the most beautiful boy I'd ever seen.

I hadn't seen her in over a year. I'd almost forgotten the way she made my stomach twist into knots.

She'd broken my heart. Crushed it into a million little pieces until it looked more like canned dog food than a vital organ. Now here she was, asking for a second chance.

We'd been friends forever, but now I wanted more.

_____

_____

_____

_____

_____

_____

_____

_____

_____

_____

_____

_____

_____

_____

_____

_____

_____

_____

_____

_____

The kiss surprised us both.

About Batch of Books

Batch of Books is a blog dedicated to finding great books for children and teens. It features reading lists, giveaways, printables, quizzes, and other fun content.

Visit us online at www.batchofbooks.com.

If you enjoyed this book, please leave a review.

Picture Credits:

Cover front: background: Dena McMurdie, all images depositphotos—alien, heart-eyes emoji, red lips, hamburger, watermelon, poop emoji, kissy face emoji, skull, drink, whatever, donut: ikopylove, open mouth with tongue: Softulka, hearts, flowers: MisterElements, black heart: topform.

Back: all images depositphotos—hearts, flowers: misterelements, yin-yang, winking heart, peace symbol, smiling emoji: ikopylove.

Page 1: all images depositphotos—pencil: misterelements, **2:** all images depositphotos—female hand holding an apple: Croisy, **3-5:** all images depositphotos—astronaut friends, astronauts looking down hole, tentacles: studiostoks, **6-18:** all images depositphotos—circuit board pattern: spirit-alex, **19:** all images depositphotos—demonic woman: Katja87, banner: Tueris, **20-32:** all images depositphotos—gothic castle: pavelmidi, **33:** all images depositphotos—fingerprints: W1nDkh, splatters: Tawng, **34-45:** all images depositphotos—magnifying glass: urfingus, **47-59:** all images depositphotos—emojis: Aratehortua, **61:** all images depositphotos—typewriter: kite-kit, **62-73:** all images depositphotos—quill pen with inkpot: Marinka, **75:** all images depositphotos—fashion girl on street background: R_lion_O, **76-88:** all images depositphotos—starburst sketch: blue67, **89:** all images depositphotos—hand-drawn raven: Ezhevica, **90-100:** all images depositphotos—spiderweb: Dr.PAS, **101:** depositphotos—young couple in love: studiostoks, heart background: Dena McMurdie, **102-116:** hearts: Dena McMurdie, **117:** poop emoji: ikopylove.

Visit

BATCH OF BOOKS

batchofbooks.com

Made in the USA
Las Vegas, NV
27 May 2024